Emotional Intelligence for Kids

EQ Activities – Emotional Intelligence Activities

by
Samantha Wiggins

Copyright © Samantha Wiggins 2013
All Rights Reserved

Table Of Contents

About the author
The Power of Emotions
Rational and emotional thinking, two sides of the same coin
Control your emotions before they will control you!
Emotional intelligence in modern day schools
Social and emotional development of children
Some thoughts on child psychology
Interpreting the behavior of our child
Activities that can help develop socio-emotional skills
Teacher's contribution to the development of socio-emotional skills in kids
Conclusions
References

About the author

Samantha Wiggins is an established teacher with more than eight years of experience. She has been working with children in primary but also preschool in her role as public school teacher (primary/junior). After graduating the University of Illinois-Chicago, she dedicated herself to teaching young minds, shaping their understanding of life through activities, games, and a valuable set of skills acquired through study and experience.

In the last three years as a teacher, she has dedicated herself to the study of emotional intelligence. Samantha had developed a series of methods that can enhance child development through proper guidance.

She was able to put in practice and measure the impacts of her activities, on children that showed deficiencies in expressing their emotions. The results were remarkable. Kids that had difficulty talking to other students, or expressing themselves in different situations, started interacting more often, and were able to show what they felt in class.

After her role as a teacher, she took a more challenging position as a Senior Editor for Ascending Line LLC, a company specialized in career planning and development. The experienced gathered here, and the expertise gained as a teacher helped in writing this book.

"Emotional Intelligence for Kids: How to raise emotional intelligence in children through games, and activities", has been received with great interest by fellow teachers and parents alike.

The Power of Emotions

Emotions have a strong influence on our lives whether we like it or not. Imagine you have left for work and, after a few hours, you want to go buy yourself some food. You reach for your pocket where you put your wallet and you cannot find it. A "mini-heart attack" sets in. Where is it? You are sure you have taken it to work; you could not have left it at home, as you remember putting it in your pocket. As you search through your things, you remember you have taken it out to pay for a co-worker's birthday. You find it. What a relief. "Thank god!" you say. However, in those brief moments, adrenaline rushed through your body creating strong emotions. I am sure you have experienced this or something similar. I know I have, countless times.

The emotions you've felt (panic/fear and relief) but also other strong ones like happiness, anger, excitement, sadness, tenderness have a major impact on our way we interact with people around us, with our friends, our colleagues or simple strangers.

If you are not aware of how people feel, you will not be able to relate to them appropriately and the chances to have a relationship of any sort with that person diminish. In addition, if you understand how you feel and how you react in certain situations, the chances to establish a connection with someone increase through empathy. You know how your colleagues will react when they hear the company is cutting salaries for all employees, because you feel it too. Comforting them is much easier when you know what they are going through. In this way, your relationships with your colleagues will improve in time.

Emotions, as well as cognitive thought, drive the actions we undertake to reach our personal goals. If your objective is to reach point B from point A the easiest and logical way to get there is a straight line. That is your cognitive thinking doing its part. Now imagine that somewhere between the two points there is a spider. Your fear kicks in and you start working on alternatives. "I could go through C to reach my destination." On the other side if the path from A to B is clear but in C however is your loving partner, which you have not seen in a long time, your obvious option will be to divert from the rational path. As you can see our emotions impact heavily on our actions and the faster we realize this, the better we will be.

Whenever your cognitive thought detects a possible threat to your well-being, a bodily reaction triggers. It releases a series of chemicals that cause your heart to pump faster, bringing oxygen to all of your muscles, heighten your senses and prepare you to physically confront your threat or run from it. Nothing out of the ordinary as these exact triggers, have helped humankind survive in case of a threat. This is how evolution prepared us for dealing with danger.

Coming back to modern times, a confrontation with a student that ignores your authority will cause an emotional response as strong as if you were physically threatened. Even though your instincts will be to fight or flee, you will rarely need for any of them in most situations.

Fear is not the only emotion that can influence our actions:

- Disgust - can help you avoid unpleasant even dangerous things that can harm you
- Happiness - can inhibit negative emotions and guide your thoughts toward a more optimistic and creative approach
- Worry - can help you better prepare your plans, by going through each potential risk and finding a solution
- Surprise - gives you a more open way to approach and look at new things

Rational and emotional thinking, two sides of the same coin

Being in touch with the emotions of others can improve your results by a whole lot. Cognitive thinking provides you with a great deal of information regarding a person; however, it is not the whole picture. Emotional intelligence can complete this picture by explaining why a certain behavior occurs in a person. As a teacher or parent, you will often need to provide feedback to your children when they do wrong or behave inappropriately. However, you will need to have a complete view of the situation (both rational and emotional).

Think about this scenario:

Julie, your 2nd grade student, has had a poor performance in the last couple of days. Her attention has not been in class and her actions reflect that. She has interrupted you a couple of times now and you are starting to grow impatient with her behavior. What do you do?

If you were to listen to your rational, fact driven side, you will be tempted to provide some form of punishment (more homework, a rebuke in front of the class or even send a letter home to her parents). Is this the best approach?

By taking Julie aside and talking to her separately, you will find the root of the problem. It is not laziness or indifference toward school activities the issue, but rather something of a more personal nature. Her mother was spending less time with her after school to help her prepare as she had taken a more time consuming job. It was necessary to support the household payments but it had a major effect on Julie's school performance. The little girl was missing guidance.

Sadly, this is a common thing nowadays as more and more families have difficulties with loans, mortgage, rent, or other monthly payments.

Having understood the background, do you still think a punishment was the best answer? A proper course of action would be spending some additional time with Julie after class to help fill the missing gap that caused her to go astray. In time and with proper methods she can become independent enough to compensate for this loss.

By understanding the emotional status of a person you will improve your results either by delaying a negative feedback until the person is calmer and more receptive, or to provide support if needed.

Emotions are not always our ally in human interactions. Situations when a strong emotional response triggers an aggressive behavior can prove challenging to our day-to-day job; they may even damage the relationship we have with people. Expressing emotions might come easy for some but others will have difficulties with them. Statistically speaking, females tend to do better on this area than men. Keep this in mind.

Another scenario to think of:

Other classmates have constantly picked on Jim, your 3rd grade student. They have been pushing him in the hallway or kicking him while the teacher was writing on the blackboard, with the back towards them. This has been going for some time and the pressure reached alarming levels. You did not suspect much of this, but at some point Jim snapped and pushed one of the bullies, which got a sprained ankle. Was this the right solution for Jim? Of course not, however the situation could have been avoided.

Jim needed to learn to express his emotions with ease. That way, you could have found out that some of the kids have been picking on him and informed their parents. Left unattended, this emotional stress has lead to an unfortunate event.

Teach your class the power of emotions! Search for activities and games that you can play with them and in the same time, help enhance their understanding and control. A few chapters forward, we will be going over some activities and games. You should however try to find additional resources to complete them. I will provide you with a series of reads I have found useful if you want to dig deeper into the child psychology subject and how emotions affect child development.

Control your emotions before they will control you!

You might be unaware but your emotional state affects everything you do. Whether it is your decisions and actions, your interactions with other people or performance on the job, emotions rule most of our life. How many times have you taken a different decision than usual, just because you were in a happier more positive mood? I know I am willing to go shopping with my wife whenever I get a raise or a bonus at work….and she knows it too :) I do not do this usually so my emotional state affects this directly.

Do you remember the times you have taken your anger on someone else? Was he/she the reason? No! It was your feelings that caused your behavior. Even though, the rational side knows you are friends with that person, emotional side takes over sometimes. That is how powerful emotions are. We have all heard of crimes of passion. There is no logical thinking behind them, only impulse, only strong emotions.

I hope that now you understand that emotions play a very important role in our day-to-day lives and that it is vital to be in tune with them. Being in tune with our emotions can help focus on the real issue of a problem. Emotions can help:

- Raise our motivation to achieve a certain goal
- Understand our own needs and the needs of others to improve how we connect with them
- Improve performance at work.

Emotional awareness is the same as the Emotional Intelligence quotient or EQ. People with high EQ are experiencing a happier and more fulfilling life. Below are the skills and abilities associated with an emotional intelligent person. We will go through each one and explain. Consider them as individual assignments. Go through each one and think about how you would rate yourself in relation to that area.

Emotional Awareness

This skill enables you to be in touch with your emotions and be able to perceive the emotions of the people you most often interact. Without it, you will not identify how your decisions are affected and how the actions you make are the result of how you feel.

Manage Emotions Effectively

The ability to control your emotions is vital when it comes to human interactions. No matter how upset, angry, or exhilarated you feel, keeping a calm, cool attitude towards an issue and/or person is a huge victory. To be able to respond calmly to a person who lost his temper is disarming; it is the best solution by far. Anger builds on anger and so if you were to answer with the same attitude you will only pile up on that.

Good Communications Skills

Being able to understand how people feel will give you a great advantage over others. You will understand where they come from when they show a certain behavior and being able to relate with them can earn you their trust and aid in building a good relationship.

Relating positively and with integrity with different people

Understanding the emotions each person goes through and showing empathy can increase the chances of more open interactions in the future. Maintain a good degree of trust as some people will consider this area quite sensitive. Respecting other people's feelings will be a proof of your integrity and will add more appreciation from people.

Self-motivation

Being able to channel your emotions can prove to be a strong and compelling drive towards your objectives. Feeling frustrated about how a process is managed can force you to take action and gain responsibility at work. This will ultimately improve your work perception as you improve the process.

Strong intuition

A high EQ person can build a good sense of intuition, as it will encompass data that is not available to every person, for example, an analytical person. How is your sense of intuition?

Emotional intelligence in modern day schools

The ever-increasing complexity of society makes cognitive intelligence, most commonly assessed in the context of education, not enough to solve everyday problems and the socio-emotional integration of future generations. There is a tendency for the current generation of children to have more emotional problems than in the past. They are lonely and depressed, angry and intemperate, more emotional and more likely to suffer from anxiety; more impulsive and aggressive.

It is noticeable that the school curriculum treats the emotional education of students with lesser importance, truly undervaluing it. Schools often enforce a mechanical approach when it comes to learning (kids learning their assignments „by heart"). Therefore it is required a new vision on what schools can offer students, so that they can better adapt to contemporary realities.

Social studies have shown the results of this system - a system that values good grades and outstanding results. It is clearly the direct approach towards greatness in a specific field. This system must complement with activities and assignments that help raise the EQ of children. All modern families take pride in the results of their children. However, they undervalue the emotional aspect of intelligence. The social interactions that can help a child blossom and develop skills receive no guidance. These interactions will help him in the future to live a fulfilling life.

In 1920, E. L. Thorndike identifies, apart from academic intelligence, a different kind of intelligence that defines the social intelligence as the "ability to understand and work with women and men, boys and girls - to behave wisely in human relations ".

Meanwhile a series of studies related to this discovery have multiplied, so in the '80s, we name a new type of intelligence called "social intelligence", which means the ability to master the personal emotions and of others, to differentiate them together and use this information to guide the thinking and action.

The first to use the term "emotional intelligence" was Wayne Leon Payne in 1985. Thus appears the first definition: "Emotional intelligence is a skill that involves a creative relationship with the state of fear, pain, and desire.

Therefore, emotional intelligence is the personal ability to identify and efficiently manage the emotions in relation to the one's personal goals (career, family, education, etc.). Its objective is to achieve them with minimal inter and intra-personal conflicts.

Social and emotional development of children

Socio-emotional development concerns the onset of a child's social life, his ability to establish and maintain interactions with adults and children. Emotional development refers especially to the children's ability to perceive and express emotions, understand and respond to the emotions of others, and self-awareness development, crucial for this area. Correlated with self-awareness the child develops a self-image, shaping the learning process.

Social development means:
- improving interaction skills with adults and children of similar ages;
- acceptance and respect for diversity;
- Encouraging pro-social behavior;

Emotional development includes:
- Identifying and understanding emotions;
- developing self-concept;
- emotional control;

Objectives and practices to be encouraged

Studies show that children who have developed social skills will better adapt to the school environment. The objectives pursued by teachers or parents that want to develop socio-emotional skills in preschool and young school children should be to:

1. form responsible adults and able to adopt a positive discipline
2. create a socio-emotional climate of trust in themselves and others
3. encourage students to recognize and express emotions

4. integrate children in the community by initiating conversation and game
5. cooperate with other children in order to accomplish different tasks or find solutions to problems
6. promote assertive communication and conflict mediation techniques
7. carry out practical activities which aims to develop social-emotional skills in preschool and school children
8. use a sense of balance as an important resource to decrease anxiety, concern, fear and negative feelings
9. support the ability to practice emotional awareness, to understand and appreciate the feelings of others
10. encourage the manifestation of a flexible, generous, compassionate attitudes

Mayer, Salovey and another colleague, David Caruso, define emotional intelligence as "the ability to perceive and express emotions, assimilate emotion into thought, understand and reason with emotions and to regulate their own emotions and those of others. (Mayer Cobb, 2000).

In his book "Emotional Intelligence," Daniel Goleman (1995, 2001) explores the emotional competencies and demonstrates that social and emotional skills can develop under proper guidance. Children involved in such programs may benefit from short and long-term benefits like well being, performance, and success in life. He identifies five elements that make up emotional intelligence:

Self-awareness - identifying and understanding emotions, awareness of emotions that change, understanding the difference between thoughts, emotions and behaviors, confidence, understanding the consequences of behaviors in terms of emotions.

Self-monitoring (managing emotions) - impulse control, anger management, desire for truth, conscientiousness, adaptability, innovation, discipline.

Motivation - setting and meeting goals, optimism and hope in the face of obstacles and failures, initiative and the desire to succeed, perseverance, dedication.

Empathy - the willingness to put yourself "in other people's shoes"; cognitive and affective; to demonstrate care, attention, and respect; understanding the needs and perspectives of others; understanding diversity.

Management of social relationships (social skills) - establishing and maintaining relationships (friends), conflict resolution, cooperation, collaboration, ability to work in teams, communication, influence, leadership

Some thoughts on child psychology

The knowledge of emotions involves identifying them and the feelings that develop in different life situations but also expressing them coherently in a given context. The difficulties in understanding, in expressing them or misunderstanding of what we transmit can often generate conflicts. Social and emotional development of preschoolers and young schoolchildren involves learning social roles and ways of interaction with different people.

School kids face assertion of their identity, self-discovery, and integration into society. Now, child's horizon widens outside of the family universe by including the school. During this time, the child becomes more independent of his family and his main concerns are about his friends and relationships with teachers and peers.

During this age, children express their emotions and feelings, have a more elaborate way of thinking, and begin to compare themselves with other children of the same age. A positive relationship with parents encourages the child to feel safe enough to venture outside their comfort zone - generally young school kids are adventurous and confident about their capabilities.

The main challenge of small children is the integration in the school, in the family and among his friends. By the age of 10, most children say they are not interested in dealing with children of the opposite sex, but often change their behavior in interactions with them.

Freud called this stage of psychosocial development the „dormant phase" (ages 6 to 11 years) in which child sexuality is "stagnant", paying particular attention to learning. His experiences, phobias, and past conditionings had already formed many of the attitudes and feelings of the child. Some of these behaviors can and, most of the time, will re-appear later in his life.

According to the stages of psychosocial development conceived by Erikson, the average schooling corresponds to the conflict: Diligence versus Inferiority. Diligence is the feature that makes a child to become proficient in a certain area. Children who are aware of the satisfaction of school accomplishments will be able to resolve successfully this conflict, but failure will lead to a sense of inferiority and therefore a state of "inertia".

For Erikson this period is essential for developing self-confidence - if they are encouraged and commended by parents and teachers, children are more persistent and will be motivated to carry out the duties. If parts are ridiculed and punished, young scholars will feel inferior.

At this age, there is a temperamental redefinition of the school kid and a remodeling of character traits, which generally receive their influence from the media figures and child's entourage. In this stage of development appears a strong feeling of belonging to the group and social community of which the child is part.

Comparison with classmates determines children to give more, to be proud of their accomplishments. Young scholar's communication skills grow as their cognitive, psychological, and social skills develop.

Emotional self-regulation in kids

In preschool and primary school, the child acquires an essential skill for further development i.e. emotional self-regulation (control of their emotions and desires). This involves the ability to initiate, to restrain, or to modulate physiological processes, thoughts and behaviors related to emotions to achieve individual goals (Thompson, 1990).

Preschoolers can identify different ways of interpreting the events in an attempt to make them harmless; through discussions with others, they can share their feelings and listen to the interpretations of others (Schaffer, 2007).

Therefore, in order to regulate negative emotions preschooler already use behavioral strategies (distraction through the game), cognitive strategies (moving thoughts away from the situation, consider things in a more positive light) or verbal (discussing emotions with others, reflecting on them).

<u>Developing self awareness during class</u>

Self-awareness, which is the image that forms on children about themselves, continues to develop during this period. A preschooler describes himself in clear terms; the description includes physical features or activities that he practices. Otherwise, young children are seen more in terms of appearance and possessions (i.e. I have blue eyes, I have a bike) and the actions they can take (i.e. I know how to skate, I help mom with shopping). Unlike older students, which are more realistic in terms of themselves, preschoolers describe themselves in optimistic terms, mentioning only positive traits. Lockhart (2002) says about the optimism of children it is beneficial because it helps in learning, maintaining motivation in continuing tasks that initially failed.

It is important to mention how preschoolers make judgments about the private nature of self, namely that preschoolers don't have yet a clear distinction between their own feelings (internal) and the behavior which they exhibit in public (Schaffer, 2007).

<u>The role of emotional intelligence in the child's educational success</u>

Emotions are crucial in the development of human personality. Specialists argue that emotional intelligence and the child's ability to relate and establish relationships with others is the key to school and life success. Many parents do not understand yet that the academic performance of children has very little to do with the baby's ability to read at an early age or solve equations prematurely. The mind is essential in developing an intelligent and resourceful child, but emotions have also an important role regarding life success. Those responsible for training and educating the mind and emotions are mainly the children's parents. The "training" of children's emotions, feelings, and mind starts since the baby's birth.

In other words, the way we treat our child, give him the attention, the patience you show to help him overcome problems, communication, the disciplined style that you apply, all contribute to the child's emotional development - crucial to educational success. Based on a child's emotional and social skills you can determine whether he will have the best chances of being successful at a later stage in life.

Here are the main elements on which the child's success depends:

- Trust in their own strength
- The power of control and self-control
- Intent (desire, perseverance, the need to put their mark on some things or issues and to solve them)
- Curiosity
- Communication (the desire to communicate, to need to establish relationships with others, to express feelings, beliefs, emotions through words)
- Cooperation -ability to share things, to wait their turn, "teamwork", adapting personal needs to the needs of a group
- Involvement (ability to involve understand others and be understood).

In conclusion, not the child's ability to read or do calculations is essential for learning and school success, but rather the ability to know how to learn things and cope with the emotional challenges.

The signs of an emotionally intelligent child

Social studies prove that some children become better performing adults from a professional and social standpoint. On the other hand, children with a strong educational knowledge, highly competent and with very good school results, fail to have friends. They are not satisfied with their careers and personal life and suffer from depression; some of them become unhappy of their day-to-day lives. What makes the difference is a certain level of development of social and emotional skills.

Here are some suggestions for the development of emotional and social skills in schools. <u>Self-knowledge</u> - the whole "arsenal" of ways, ego discovers itself and becomes stronger. <u>Empathy</u> - knowing your measure, the measure of others and of the situation you are in. <u>Communication</u> - cultivating quality relationships has a positive effect on the environment; promote assertiveness. <u>Cooperation / leadership</u> - effective leadership is not based on domination, but on the art of helping people to work together toward common goals.

Eight signs of an emotionally intelligent child:

1. has the ability to speak freely about what he feels
2. knows and identifies his own emotions and of those around him;
3. easily communicates with those around him, is open to dialogue;
4. knows how to control negative feelings and impulses
5. is motivated (discovers the pleasure behind certain activities and is geared towards performance or success)
6. adapts easily to new situations
7. has friends and easily establishes relationships with those around him
8. is able to impose their own preferences and ask questions

Interpreting the behavior of our child

Faced with the same situation, adults (parents and teachers) have different reactions to the same behavior of a child.

For example, faced with the behavior of throwing toys, adults react differently depending on the interpretation that they make. "This kid does not understand that he mustn't slam his toys! He does this intentionally to annoy me!" They feel angry and have a high probability to react with aggressive behavior (snatch the toys from their hand or raise their voice). Those who give a different interpretation to this behavior - "the child is bored, doesn't know how to play or he wants to draw his parents' attention" remain calm and will guide the child to other activities.

The reactions that adults face regarding this kind of behavior may differ depending on the interpretation and meanings that they offer. The same type of behavior causes various reactions even in the same person at different times, depending on the context in which the perceived behavior occurs.

Child's behavior is the result of his learning experiences (child logical thinking is often within the limits of a simple equation: do X – obtain Y. Child behavior is a reflection of the skills that he has at some point. Inappropriate behaviors hide a lack of skill set and reflect the need for new learning within a new context.

Examples of emotional regulation in class

I have put together a few examples and scenarios from which we can learn what are the best ways to react to certain situations. These examples should be taken as food for thought and are here to guide you in similar scenarios:

Learning example no.1

The teacher asks the children to present their notebooks to check if they had done the assignment. Matthew begins to sing loudly and beat the desk with his fists.

A. The reaction of the adult is based only on the fact that he has an obstructive student that defied his request.

What does the teacher think?

He sees the child's behavior as a defiance against his authority and as an attack toward him.

How does the teacher feel?

He feels the fear that the other children will copy his model and his authority will be affected. Depending on his learning experiences and his character traits, there can be several strategies to address this behavior.

How does he react?

- Aggressive behavior (child quarrel, punishment, labels him in front of the class as someone who disturbs the class, uses a high tone and inappropriate words)
- Avoidance behavior (tells him to go outside to cool down, lets him do what he wants)

What does the child learn from this experience?

That the use of inappropriate behavior can help him avoid involvement in school tasks. That he can get the attention needed through inappropriate behaviors.

B. The reaction of the adult is congruent to the child's need to learn

How does the adult interpret the child's behavior?

The teacher sees the child's behavior as the result of a learning experience. He learned to use this strategy to avoid involvement in the school activities and to avoid the unpleasant consequences of the discovery that he has not studied or prepared his assignment.

How's does the teacher feel?

He maintains composure and addresses the issue as a problem-solving situation.

How does he respond to the child's behavior?

Acts in accordance with the learning objectives

<u>Learning Objectives</u>

- Respond to adult's request (present assignment)
- Manifest behaviors suited to the school (to respond when asked to participate in school activities with colleagues)

How can the adult respond according to the learning objectives?

- Observe and identify the emotion by saying "I see you're anxious"
- Encourage emotional expression, "What happened?"
- Calls the rule "the rule says to talk only when you are asked"
- Apply logical consequence for violating the rule (for disturbing the class and talking without being asked you will receive a warning)
- Check assignment
- Talk to the student in private and use a calm tone. Walk with the student outside the classroom and a discussion and discuss the matter in a calm and assuring way. Public reprimands and threats, cold and authoritative tone, discussions and arguments in front of the class have as a result an increase in aggressive behavior.
- Identify together with the child solutions to improve the situation - How can we solve the problem otherwise - to complete the assignment

the next day, to stay half an hour after school to complete it

Intervention in this case, when other methods do not work, involves seeking the help of his parents.

A child's behavior is monitored daily, based on specific indicators:

- he writes and reads together with his colleagues
- stays in his seat throughout the duration of the class
- raises his hand when he wants to talk and responds if asked

Learning example no.2

The teacher asks a question in front of the class. A student answers without permission.

The teacher's response to the inappropriate behavior is tied to how he explains and interprets the behavior. What he thinks about the student's inappropriate actions, influences what he will do in response. Whether he does something or not, the teacher sends a message to the students (if the aggressive behavior goes unnoticed the child might learn that it is possible to break the rules without assuming any consequences).

A. The response is aggressive and reproves the child in front of the class

How does the adult interpret the child's behavior?

He considers his reaction as a disturbance that calls for punishment.

How does the teacher feel?

He feels anger, annoyance, displease.

How does he react?

He threatens to kick him out of the class if he does not learn to raise his hand. Uses a negative body language (he points, fixes his eyes), starts a battle for power with the student ("You will do as I say because I say so!")

What do children learn from this experience?
- to respond in the same way in a similar situation (without waiting to be called)
- to respond by aggressive behaviors when angry (to threaten in similar situations, just as his teacher did)
- to raise their voice on top of others (students learn that this is how someone can be noticed and can solve a problem)

B. The reaction of the adult is based on the child's need to learn

How does the adult interpret the child's behavior?

Considers that the un-called answer is caused by the child's desire to show that he prepared for class, or because he has an attention deficit

How does the teacher feel?

He maintains calm

How does he react?

His reactions encourage learning to positive behavior. He does not punish the child nor does he reprove him. Instead, the teacher talks to him and tries to understand the reasons behind his behavior.

Learning Objective

To structure the content and create an environment that encourages waiting (i.e. having a class play where everyone must learn to wait their turn and then speak their mind... role-playing, theatre plays...etc)

How can the adult respond according to the learning objectives?

1. He reminds him the class rules: "to wait being asked before he answers." Reminding the class rules avoids attracting discussion in the personal space. (avoids entering into discussions like "I do not want it, or you'll do as I want")
2. Establishes eye contact with the student who violated the rule when talks to him. If the student sits down, the teacher must sit next to him so that they are at the same level. (this is done in order to avoid to speak with him from a superior position that will cause him to feel intimidated)
3. Talks to the student using a calm tone (avoid public admonitions and threats, a cold and authoritative tone that are designed to increase aggressive behavior)
4. Catches an event when the student has followed the rules and praises him
5. Considers only the answers received from students who have complied with this rule.
6. Praises cooperation in any situation in which it occurs with the student.

You should do some monitoring at an interval of 5 - 10 minutes, depending on the case. For every 10 minutes the child followed the rules, he gets a small reward. In this way, the child receives a reward for good behavior.

Activities that can help develop socio-emotional skills

The objectives of the activities I will share with you in this chapter will provide you a good start toward your kid's emotional development. Think of them as tools that help kids to develop a strong vocabulary on expressing emotions. They learn that it is normal to have emotions, to be able to distinguish between physical pain from the emotional one, to differentiate between enjoyable and unpleasant emotions, to understand that it is better to express emotions. Kids will start to recognize the difference between real danger and fear and to discuss ways in which we can face fear.

Note: some activities can only be done in groups as they require human relationships to achieve their goals.

1. The Wheel of Emotions

Preparation: 30 minutes

Activity duration: 2-3 minutes per child

For this activity, you will need some preparations done beforehand. Cut a circle of cardboard 20 inches in diameter. Find the center and draw 13-14 quadrants. Write on each quadrant an emotion or mood. Here are some examples to start with but if you feel a certain emotion needs more attention in your class or family feel free to add it: Restless, Unhappy, Sad, Happy, Aggressive, Furious, Angry, Frustrated, Upset, Certain, Worried, Scared, Angry, Confused.

Create a stand with an axle on which the wheel can turn and place it in front of the children. The stand should also have a pointer to identify the emotion when the wheel stops turning.

Ask someone to come and spin the wheel and tell a story from their experience when they manifested the emotion written on the wheel.

The goal is to help children express what they feel. It is possible that some students will not be able to express clearly, what an emotion is, but we can offer them alternatives to distinguish between positive emotions (good) and negative ones (bad).

You can help them by providing some examples: you dropped a tooth, you learn to read, you lose a book, parents punished you because you lied, you learned to ride a bicycle, you made a new friend, you've been stung by a bee, a mosquito bit you etc. Remember that this activity has the purpose to identify the emotion not judge them in any way. This helps raise emotional self-awareness in your children.

2. Who am I? Who are you?

Preparation: 10 minutes

Activity duration: 15 minutes

Take a sheet of paper and draw 4-5 bubbles in a circle and another one in the center similar to the below image:

Print one for each child. You will need an even number if not you can use the student without pair to give an example to the class. Ask children to write the name of their pair in the middle and then think of the emotions that person makes them feel and write them down. The exercise encourages kids to express their emotions in a controlled environment. The teacher or parent can mediate some potential arguments if any.

Students will learn to differentiate between pleasant emotions and unpleasant ones. We can have control over unpleasant emotions by telling ourselves that the problems can be solved, and just because we feel bad now, does not mean that we will always feel that way.

3. A matter of perspective

Preparation: none in advance

Duration: 10 minutes

Tell your kids the following story:

"Mom and dad came home from the market but forgot to buy some eggs for the cake she was supposed to bake. It is Mike's birthday. His sister, Stacy, has just come home from school as well.

Dad is upset that he needs to drive mom to the supermarket instead of watching the game

Mom feels guilty as she had made the shopping list, but forgot the milk

Mike is sad, as he wanted to spend the whole day with his entire family, eat cake, and play with his sister.

Stacy is happy as she can accompany her parents to the market to buy some more strawberries - her favorites."

Give the children some other examples and ask them to identify how people impacted by the event feel.

- the fire alarm goes off during classes
- your brother/sister/friend has won a sports competition (chess, swimming, football)
- Dad built a small swimming pool in the middle of the yard where your mom used to plant vegetables.

You can also improvise and bring some scenarios that are more familiar to your kids so that they can relate better.

The purpose of the exercise is to improve understanding of emotions in others, a crucial skill as it builds toward a highly empathic person, who will most likely adapt very well in every environment.

4. Friends stick together
Preparation: 15 minutes
Duration: 20-30 minutes

Cut some sheets of paper in small pieces 3 inches in length and 1 in width. Make around 10 for each child you want to participate in the activity. Get some paper glue as well.

Tell your class/kids about the importance of friends in everyone's life, how they can help you in need, comfort you when you are sad and laugh with you when you are happy. Ask them to think about their friends and write something about them on the paper slips you have made in advance. The emphasis is on what they feel when thinking about that person.

Now ask them to fold the paper twice so that you get three equal areas. Imagine a square sliced in three equal areas.

With the slip folded add some glue on the short edges and glue the two sides together to make a loop. Repeat with the next friend but now add the previous loop, before you glue the two edges. Make some more and each child will have a small chain of friends in their hands.

You can use paper of various colors if you want to suggest variety. Kids will soon discover that they had more friends than previously thought, as they become aware of the length of the chain. Ask your children to identify which emotions their friends reminded them.

5. Choices

Preparation: 5 minutes

Duration: throughout a few days

Ask your children to pay attention to their actions and ask them to write their opinions on them. Evaluate whether the decision made were responsible ones or not. Ask them to write the opposite of their actions to enhance the comparison. Below a guideline for them to follow:

1. Describe the action:
2. Was your action a responsible one?
3. What were the reactions of others?

4. What have you learned from this?
5. What would be the opposite action?
6. How would this action affect others?

After a few days gather all assignments and discuss them in front of the class. That way you can set examples on how a responsible action can have far more benefits regarding the relationships with other people, friends or family.

6. Be Flexible!

Preparation: none

Duration: 15 minutes

Explain to your children/class the importance of being flexible when interacting or dealing with an unpleasant event. Surpassing an obstacle is much easier with the proper attitude. A positive and open one will get you more ideas and be able to find the best solution to the current situation. Read the story below to emphasize on the message.

"George and Jessica have been planning a trip with their kids to a nearby forest. They prepared the supplies they needed for camping, bought marshmallows and brought dad's guitar. However, the night before they wanted to go a thunderstorm hit. The weather was terrible; they could not go hiking, make a barbeque, or sit by the fire playing songs.

George was upset as he planned the so-called escape for a couple of weeks now and has been dreaming about it ever since. The kids were crying, realizing that they could not go this weekend.

Mom saved the day by suggesting a different type of activity. She had read in a newspaper that there was a comic book and video game convention in the next town. Her kids were enjoying superhero movies and played video games. They had so much fun watching all the costumes, bought posters and enrolled in competitions with other kids. It was a blast!"

Test your flexibility by underlining your option from each of the following scenarios:

1) You and your parents are going to the cinema to watch the movie you have wanted to see in a long time, however when you reach the cinema you find out that all the tickets have been sold out. Do you:

- Start to kick and scream that you want to see this movie ONLY!
- Look at the cinema schedules to see if you can book some tickets for next time.
- You get upset and ask your parents to go home, as you do not want to see anything else.

2) You are expecting your cousins over to play with you, however in the last minute they call you to cancel as they are grounded and cannot leave their house. Do you:

- Get upset and ask them not to call you in the next days
- Let them know you feel sorry and that you can play some other time
- Ask your mother if you can go to their house and play instead.

3) You are playing a board game with your friends and you lose a series of games. Do you:

- Focus harder to try to catch up
- Give up as your chances of winning have diminished
- Ruin the board game so that no one can play further.

7. Decisions, decisions!

Preparation: none

Duration: 10 minutes

Making decisions is a very important part of a self-functioning adult that is able to make a clear distinction between right and wrong. Follow the below list of actions and ask your child to check which one he would do and which he would not:

1. Send your mother a birthday card!
2. Push someone in response to an insult
3. Thank your grandpa for taking you to the zoo
4. Lie when mom asks you if you have done your homework
5. Do the chores mom has requested from you
6. Tell someone you do not like them

Remember to discuss with the class the situation when a child has chosen the wrong decision. If someone says, 2, 4 or 6 you should explain what the correct decision is and why.

8. Puppet play

Preparation: 0 / 1hour

Duration: 1hour

This activity has two parts. One where you build your materials with the class and the second where you make scenarios to play with the hand puppets.

For the first part, each child should have:

- *colored sock*
- *2 large buttons and a smaller one*
- *Some wool threads...black or colored is up to them*
- *Needle and some fine thread*

Ask each child to sew the two large buttons to the sock so that they resemble the eyes. Then do the same with the other button in between the other two. This will be the nose. Get the threads and sew them on top of the sock as hair. It is a fun activity for them as they are free to choose all the materials. You can have the activity during the crafting class if you have one.

Part two - You will ask the children to imagine a conversation between two characters. Take some chairs to mask where the children sit and have a blanket cover them. The stage is set. Some scenarios to consider:

- *Two brothers fighting for the same toy*
- *Two kids sharing ice cream in the park*
- *Son trying to convince dad to go camping*
- *3 kids in the playground start to play together.*

9. Dear Diary

Preparation: none

Duration: throughout the school year

Encourage your children to express their emotions through writing. Ask them to buy a small notebook and start writing their experiences. Ask them to make a habit of writing at least once a week. That way they will not forget the happy moments they experience. Remember them to write also about more upsetting event. That way they will be able to identify it and maybe prevent it in the future.

Let them know that they are the only ones that will read them and that they can if they want to hide it from everyone else. It is a good and healthy exercise for kids to express emotions through writing.

10. Relax!

Ask your children to think of events when they were stressed or uncomfortable. Here are some examples that I have found some kids have difficulties:

- *speaking in front of class*
- *talking to a colleague*
- *talking to an adult*
- *dancing in front of someone*
- *singing in front of people*
- *taking a test*

Make them write down two situations when they felt stressed.

Ask them to answer the following questions:

- *What can you do to make it better during the experience? (Take deep breaths, focus)*
- *How can you prevent it? (Prepare better, practice in front of the mirror)*

Teacher's contribution to the development of socio-emotional skills in kids

It is crucial to provide children with a learning environment to develop their emotional and social skills. Dr. James Comer, 1999 finds particularly relevant the impact of a supportive environment, at home and at school, for the social and emotional development of the child. It is a huge difference for the children who grow up in a culture that causes emotional and social development.

1. Integrate activities to develop social and emotional skills in the daily schedule. (I.e. emotions of the day, teamwork in problem solving)

2. Prove your students a socially and emotionally intelligent behavior through your actions.

3. Be receptive toward the events that happen naturally in class: moments when you notice a changing in their moods and dispositions, conflicts, acts of concern for others, respect and attention!

4. Encourage discussions about the expression of emotional and social skills developed in your classroom! For example, a display of emotional vocabulary, a student gives a compliment to another colleague or to his teachers, or topics about which they want to talk.

5. Keep a journal to reflect on your emotions and encourage the children you work with to have one as well to monitor their emotions, both positive and negative.

6. Provide support to students in evaluating emotions and feelings: teaching them to classify words that define emotions, find appropriate words for their feelings, and start by expressing emotions, discussions about feelings.

7. Respect the feelings of students: ask them how they feel, ask them what they want before you act, think how your activities will make the students feel; what type of feelings creates a positive environment for learning.

8. Empower them! Ask them how they feel and what they need to do to feel better, teach them to solve their own problems using empathy, compassion, and mutual respect for the feelings of others.

9. Avoid labeling and critical judgments: topics as being good / bad, nice / rude, beautiful / ugly, etc.,

10. Identify the emotional state of the students at the beginning of the day or during the day and shift them towards positive, creative thoughts through ice breaking activities.

11. Allow time to talk about emotions / feelings associated with learning situations. Discuss with students the responsibility of emotions (reactions, consequences)

12. Offer prizes, rewards and sanctions as well (positive discipline).

13. Focus yourself on the things they enjoy doing! (Passions / hobbies, favorite activities) Do not judge them when they express what they feel!

14. Give specific feedback, depending on how he feels and how each student behaves. Identify and appreciate the smallest progress..

Conclusions

Social skills contribute substantially to an efficient adaptation and integration in the environment we live in. Through interactions with others, we achieve individual goals. We reach them not only through pure cognitive thought but also through emotions, through human relationships that push us forward. Without emotions and relationships, our lives are meaningless.

Thus, a child's ability to develop relationships with other children until the age of 6 years and above is often more important than having a high IQ. Some kids bloom late and some early, their cognitive processes start to kick in at different stages in life. Emotional intelligence however is something that kids must practice and develop starting kindergarten. The process of developing social and emotional skills begin as early as the first years of life, which is why the quality of interactions with others are crucial (parents, other family members, other adults in the kindergarten, school, group friends / colleagues, etc..).

According to research, adaptation is conditioned by the ability to establish relationships with other children, and by the ability to make friends. To function effectively as adults and be independent you are required to have a set of social and emotional skills.

Some of the risks of poorly developed social and emotional skills in children:

- Behavioral problems (deviance and juvenile delinquency, aggression and violence, school dropout, integration difficulties in a group, rejecting others, isolation)
- Emotional problems (depression, anxiety)
- learning problems (decreased performance, adaptation school requirements)
- Lack of self-confidence

In this context, teachers and family are responsible of child development. Adults need to be proactive in creating an environment of openness, honesty, and acceptance in order to meet different personalities and temperaments, and diverse cultural backgrounds. It is important to learn and enjoy together in an environment that provides support for all children.

References

I have put together a list of books that to me are valuable in terms of information, books that had helped me in my research throughout the years. Parents or teachers should use the first selection of books in the education of their children. The second part has theoretical knowledge, for people who want to dig deeper into this subject and understand the concepts and principles of emotional intelligence.

For reading with your children:

- Little Teddy Bear's Happy Face, Sad Face, by Linda Offerman
- The Way I Feel, by Janan Cain
- Today I Feel Silly: And Other Moods That Make My Day by Jamie Lee Curtis
- A to Z: Do You Ever Feel Like Me?, by Bonnie Hausman
- Glad Monster, Sad Monster, by Ed Emberley and Anne Miranda
- Double-Dip Feelings, by Barbara Cain
- The Hurt, by Teddi Doleski

To enrich your knowledge in the field and become a competent parent / teacher:

- The Whole-Brain Child: 12 Revolutionary Strategies to Nurture Your Child's Developing Mind by Daniel J. Siegel and Tina Payne Bryson
- Raising An Emotionally Intelligent Child by John Gottman PhD
- Emotional Intelligence: 10th Anniversary Edition by Daniel Goleman
- Emotional Intelligence 2.0 by Travis Bradberry

Thank You!